Foreward

There's something about fathers and daughters. An unexplainable bond that is magical, endearing and tough to break. Few embody it like the relationship between Yetunde (nee Bankole) and her now late Dad, Chief Bankole.

I first became aware of their special relationship in 1999. Back then, Yetunde and I were on our compulsory national youth service. We had initially met in Benue State, where we had a 3-week orientation. Months later, we found ourselves, through different routes, in Ibadan, Oyo State. Close to the end of our service year, she

recruited me to edit a book she had written on the National Youth Service Corps (NYSC). I was happy to do so.

The launch of that book in Ibadan allowed me to see how close Yetunde was to her Dad. A top-class venue, apparently paid for by her Dad, had been hired and set out. Chief and Mrs Bankole arrived at the venue regally dressed in befitting Yoruba attire. To cap it all, dignitaries from the State and Captains of Industry were present. The arrangements were so extensive that it later created a major protocol issue within the NYSC Management team in

Ibadan. In any case, when her Dad took the microphone on that august day to speak, you could feel the pride in his voice as he eulogized his daughter in ways that only a Dad could. It was moving and, decades later, remains etched in my memory bank.

I never got to meet Chief Bankole again until he sadly passed on in 2019. Yet, for weeks after, I and many of Yetunde's friends watched as she reeled out stories after stories of a lifetime with her Dad. They were stories of a beautiful life of impact; stories of a relationship that was filled with fun, happiness, counselling, path setting and character building. Each new story compelled a feeling of familiarity with a man that had lived his life well and left great memories of his time on earth.

This book is a continuation of those stories. Indeed many of the stories here were shared back then. Reading it is like reading two books in one – the abridged biography of a father on one hand and the autobiography of a daughter on the other. The reader is taken through a journey of exposition on the culture of the Yoruba people of Nigeria (one of which practices makes a child the "mother" of her father and to be treated as such); and an understanding of life growing up in a communal environment where the extended family system is as important, if not more important, than the nuclear family.

The stories are told in an entertaining way, filled with anecdotes and punch lines that are peculiarly Nigerian. For non-Nigerian readers, it will be helpful to check the Glossary to understand the nuances of some words and phrases. Wherever you fall though, this is a book that will leave you entertained, educated and reflective. Not every book can achieve those three in one go.

Chris Adetayo

Lagos, 2020

The Straw That Broke The Camel's Back

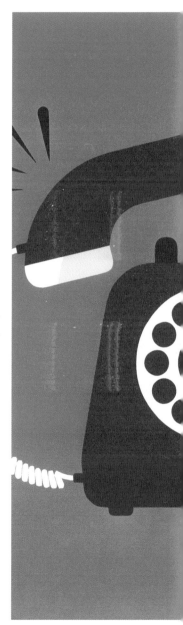

I was getting ready to go to work that morning in 'Rainchester'. The day before had been hectic and emotionally draining from trying to get dad checked into a hospital, starting with my younger sister in Nigeria ringing me whilst I was at work.

"Daddy is not waking up'
"What do you mean by that? Is he breathing?"
"Yes, he is! He is just not waking up"

I started to panic *"Pinch him, his feet, his hand, his face, everywhere"*

The rest of the day went in a blur. We had to involve several family members in Nigeria to help get him to a decent hospital. After being passed from one medical establishment to the other, they finally ended up at one of the General Hospitals about midnight. Sleep was the farthest thing from my mind and I kept my phone on throughout the night in case they needed to reach me. He survived the night, but the prognosis was not good- according to the doctors.

I got ready for work with trepidation – Is this the day I lose my dad? I naively told myself that I was ready (smh!). My sisters were already talking about mortuary. I could not tell the boys (my brothers). I walked my girls to school then proceeded to go catch the bus to work on that wet, cold morning.

At my dad's curtain call, I was at the bus stop waiting patiently (scratch that – impatiently as the bus was oddly late that morning). My big sister's call came in as I watched the bus approach my stop. My hands shaking, I said or rather asked a rhetorical question.
"He's gone, Abi?"

All I heard in response was weeping at the other end of the line.
I ran. As I ran, I called my younger brother in London and my older cousin whom I had given an update less than an hour before as I ran all the way home. I got back home, a heartbroken little girl then summoned some strength to conference call my brothers in the U.S, text my office, call/ text a few friends and family members. Then the dam broke – hard and fast. I was devastated. I was not ready – nothing could have prepared me for this – absolutely nothing.

My mind became a battlefield – I was battling conflicting thoughts in my head. 'When the bible talks about the accuser of the brethren, it ain't a joke'.

Prelude

*I became the accused - You are guilty –
You complained about the stress. This is
all your fault Yetty, You killed him – You
didn't do enough – You should have done
this- You could have done that- and so my
thoughts spiralled.*

*I tossed and turned all through the night
and forced myself to remember my dad
alive and the experiences we shared. I
smiled, laughed or cried at some of the
memories and wished he was there to talk
about the good old days.*

*"The irony of grief is that the person you
need to talk to about how you feel is the
person who is no longer here".*

To cope with the grief, I started to share
the experiences I had with my dad as
updates on my WhatsApp status while
planning his funeral. I derived strength
from the overwhelming encouragement
I received from friends and family who
were following my updates and
catching a small glimpse of who my dad
was. Some friends also shared their
personal experiences with my dad thus,
opening my eyes to awesome shades of
Jacob Oloruntoba Bankole beyond him
being my father.

So, I decided to share my daddy's

In My Father's House

stories with a much wider audience
because I am extremely proud of the
man who was my father as he took
parenting to another level. His life was
an inspiration not just to me and my
siblings but and many others in lots of
different ways.

I also share these stories for
POSTERITY. To quote a dear friend,
"Yetty, it is important that your children,
your nieces and your nephews do not
forget their Grandad and you have got
to keep him alive in them and talk
about him. Kids love hearing stories
about their family, and it gets even
more important as they get older".

These stories might be a bit of back and
forth like in the series 'This is US' where
nothing makes sense until it does.
Forgive me, I am not a writer. In fact,
my little girl corrects my prose as she's
a natural-born writer.

In the words (or music if you prefer) of
Julie Andrews, "Let's start from the very
beginning, a very good place to start".

Glossary

The style of writing I adopt in this book evidences my "Nigerian-ness" with the use of several Nigerian words/phrases/slangs. A glossary of the terms has been provided below albeit correctly or incorrectly. Hope it gives you the general gist.

Yoruba /Hausa/Igbo	The 3 Major Nigerian tribes. There's loads more.
Abi	Just a word for emphasis
Ke	No idea – In my context of use, just an exclamation
Hian	Another exclamation. Origin – Igbo Culture
Kai	And another exclamation. Origin – Hausa culture
Yee M'ogbe	I'm in trouble. But still basically an exclamation.
Yeepa	Exclamation when something serious happens.
Sha	An adjective for more emphasis
Oh	Not sure how to explain this one
O jare	Means 'Please with the added O for emphasis.
E don do	Stop
Abeg	Please (a polite addition to a request or command)
Nawaoo!	Wow! – Another Exclamation

Chai	Still exclaiming (we have many variations)
Boda	Concatenated version of Brother
Wahala	Problem or trouble
Ehn	Yes? (I think) depending on the context
Buka	Tasty Nigerian Street Food Vendor
NEPA	National Elecric Power Authority
Ko Le Werk	It won't work
Sho	What??
Sisi	Young Lady
Agbada	A loose-fitting robe worn by men in Nigeria
Danfo	A passenger bus that operates in Lagos, Nigeria
Okada	Motorcycle Taxi in Nigeria

CHAPTER 1

What's in a
Name?

For me? **Plenty**

I am number 4 and by no means the first child or the last child. I am also not the first or the last daughter.

But...I was his MOTHER!

Confused? Be patient, though some of you already know sha but let me tell the story my way – it's my story after all.

Yetunde – 'Mother has come back'
In traditional Yoruba culture, my first name is "**OrukoAmutorunwa**"- a bit of a tongue twister there. If you ain't Yoruba, DO NOT try to pronounce it.

The literal translation is 'A name brought from Heaven'
Why? I ticked all the boxes required by culture. I translate that to 'God called me by name'.

- *I had a paternal grandma*✓. *Big deal, so does everyone, right?*
- *She died* ✓
- *She had two surviving sons (one son is enough)* ✓
- *One of the sons had a heavily pregnant wife* ✓
- *The wife gave birth to a beautiful baby girl exactly a month after grandma died (The timing doesn't matter, just for my own emphasis).* ✓
- *The baby girl was the first girl born to the family after grandma died* ✓
- *So, grandma didn't actually die, she came back* ✓

Hence my first name, Yetunde.

Hian! I did not complain o.
In actual fact, I love the name and its many variations. There are major Nigerian music lyrics that quote my name and I am nodding my head to the inaudible beats of one of such songs as I type this line.

Anyway, back to the story ojare.

To further compound the matter, the two sons decided to give me my Grandma's other names. Yee M'ogbe o. Here goes:

Dorcas – Greek translation of Aramaic name Tabitha, meaning Gazelle
*Growing up, I hated this name with a passion. In my opinion, it was old and not fancy enough. It was worse whenever we went to the village, as my village people pronounced the name '**Doh – Kaa- sii** (See my life). Unfortunately, it was one of the name on my birth certificate. Years down the line, searching out who bore the name in the bible made it acceptable. I am still not overly in love with it, but I have accepted it.*

Olujuwon – God is Greater than them
I don't know who is the 'them' that God was greater than when my Grandma was born. But I am certain nobody vexed the brothers before I was born so why give me the name except to reiterate that God is greater than those who thought their mother died.

Why did they punish me like this?

It felt like I was being shown off in a 'God pass dem' kind of scenario. And my dad revelled in showing me off while he was alive.

Thankfully, I wasn't born face down or they would have probably given me grandmama's 3rd name' Ajayi. With these names, my identity at such an early age was that of a Matriarch, already being moulded by my father (son) to be a leader, a mother and a backbone.

To the sons, I was their mum indeed returned. My uncle fondly called me 'IyaTaiye' meaning Taiwo's mum as my dad was a twin at birth. My dad called me 'My Mother' when he wasn't calling me any of the other numerous nicknames I grew up with.

In hindsight, he rarely ever used my first name unless there was a 3rd party present or directly to a 3rd party. All his text messages and phones started with 'My Dear Mother' and ended with 'Your loving Son, Taiye'

Did I regularly play the 'mother 'card to get my way? Your guess is as good as mine.

CHAPTER 2

"Adatitiyoh"

———————

The chapter title is toddler speak for an actual Yoruba statement "BodaLati ti lo" (meaning Uncle Lati has gone).

It is stories like this chapter that makes me realise that I was (am) a daddy's girl through and through. I didn't even realise it until a few friends pointed this out to me after he died. They never even met my dad but apparently, I spoke about him a lot.

Rumour has it that when I was a toddler, I would keep watch over my dad once I see his driver (who had been with us so long that he had more or less become family), knowing that he had come to whisk daddy away. As you may have guessed, the driver was called Lati. And as with many Nigerian families, every older male we come across gets the 'Uncle' appendage.

Dad would promise me that he wasn't going anywhere, and I would gullibly believe him. To be on the safe side, I would climb on the sofa and watch the driver clean the car downstairs. As long as he was there, my daddy was in the house or so I thought. Besides, I hadn't seen him go out the front door so he must be inside, right?

Wrong! He would sneak out the back door into the car and the next thing I knew was the car driving away.

Haaaaa! How manage?
Someone is still telling me that my dad was inside meanwhile, the car is moving which meant 'Adatitiyoh' therefore daddy must also be gone.

Adati Gone = Daddy Gone.
I was traumatised and it was all Adati's fault that my dad left for a whole day. Maybe I resented him for that and refused to say hello to him whenever he came to the house.

I would cry and cry until I fell asleep, but the phrase became one of my many nicknames especially as BodaLati was in our lives for gazillion years. - *Happens to the best of us*.

I finally started nursery and was enrolled in a nursery school close to where daddy worked so I got to ride in the car along with him. I don't remember if I cried on the first day of nursery, but I am sure I was just so

happy to spend more time with him to even care. Until...

He forgot me in school.
Wait first, it wasn't only me (Just being dramatic). There were several of us as he had taken on the responsibility of carpooling all the neighbours' children attending the same school, as many as could fit into his Peugeot Station Wagon (lapping of course).

He was so engrossed with work that he forgot he needed to pick us up after school until about 8 pm (so the story goes). I vaguely remember being asleep at the school's gatehouse.

That singular incident led to a series of event that ended up with me being withdrawn from that school and enrolled at a school closer to home....

Moral of the story: Don't forget your child in school.

On a more serious note though; Men do not try to come between a girl and her dad, it never ends well.

CHAPTER 3

All Aboard the

Birthday Express

Birthdays in the household of my father, Jacob Oloruntoba Taiwo (JOT) was always one to remember.

He was never one for all the birthday paparazzi i.e. cards, gifts and parties but that didn't stop us from celebrating. For some reason, our house was always brimming with people which meant that the cooking pots had to be dragged out and put to good use (even without the parents). We cooked our food, bought drinks, and baked our cakes unless it was a milestone birthday. One of our neighbours was a photographer and gladly obliged our invitation to capture the day in photos.

Every year, mum would buy a birthday card and sign it 'Love Mum' then put the card at the top of our Cathode Ray Tube television (you know the one I am talking about, right?) - The brown box.

Anyway, I digress.

Once mum leaves the sitting room, daddy would walk in, pick up the card and add '& dad' after mum's words. As far as he was concerned, what belongs to her, belongs to him. This song and dance continued until ... I can't remember.

In more recent years, he started calling me at midnight, on the dot of my birthday morning without fail. He would pray from his heart, father for child and switch to child for mother. I looked forward to these calls and would deliberately not respond to anybody else until I had spoken to my dad.

The blessings of a parent – Priceless.

On my birthday in 2019, a few months before he passed away, I waited and waited. No call! I kept checking my phone all through the day. No call!

How could he forget? Even whilst I was hosting a few friends and laughing, I was

hurting inside. My dad had not called me but instead of me calling him, I sulked and pouted inside.

The following day, I called him to vent about how he forgot me and accused him of replacing me. He quietly said to me 'I am so sorry my darling, you know it's not in my character'. My annoyance dissipated once I heard how tired he was.

In hindsight, was he trying to wean me off the birthday calls? Did he know he would not be around in 2020 to wish me a happy birthday and was trying to prepare me in 2019? Who knows?

All I know is, I would never hear that voice at the other end of the phone ever again and it hurts badly. I wish I had recorded some of the calls to replay now, but I took it for granted that he would always be around to cheer me on.

CHAPTER 4

All I'm Missing

is You

If you are familiar with country music, then you probably know that the chapter title is a song by Don Williams. As I write this chapter, I am listening to this song with tears in my eyes and a smile on my face. Contradictory? Not really.

I shed tears of sadness because dad's gone but I smile because we made these memories that I share with you now.

JOT and I had a shared love for music. Sorry, I meant to say he instilled music in me from an early age so I could not but love music.

The man could sing, Chai! He had a deep baritone and sang with so much passion that you could literally see the muscles in his face bulge out. The shape of his mouth singing was also something to behold and he made a beautiful guttural sound.

A lot of people said my dad was a genius; he was smart and very intelligent. Well, I remember the ingenuity he demonstrated through music. He was a singer, songwriter, organist and choirmaster with many community songs/ anthems under his belt. He never missed an opportunity to express his music prowess and also appreciate good music.

When I was growing up, I must have been about 8/9 y/o (can't exactly remember), my dad would give me assignments to learn a specific song for the week. Our Saturday morning ritual was to put the record on and sing the song for the week together - him with his deep baritone and me with my developing voice. I didn't know this then, but the activity possibly helped me to learn how to memorise lyrics super- fast.

As young as I was, he taught me to listen and sing the perfect harmony. In so doing, he trained my music ears (not musical ear syndrome) but a good ear for music. I think I can boast of having "Golden Ears" (you make my point if you don't know what that means (lol) – don't run to google.

We must have gone through all of Don Williams' songs then we moved on to Abba (Dancing Queen was a favourite), Jim Reeves and other amazing singers. It was like a rite of passage to him– you cannot learn to sing without singing good music.

CHAPTER 5

The Best Laid

Plan....

Towards one summer break, I had been told that a close family friend was coming to visit. Uncle Sonny lived in London. We had visited him several times so when I heard he was coming to town I was so excited. I had a plan that I was willing to share with all my friends in school.

I was moving to London to live with Uncle Sonny. I was 7 years old.

Summer holiday slowly rolled by and school closed then Uncle Sonny arrived as planned. Yay! Of course, he came with lots of goodies, but I was not interested... I had a plan that I was slowly setting into motion.

A few days before Uncle Sonny was due to return, I boldly declared to JOT that I was going back with him. JOT looked at me and said OK. What?? I was ready for a debate and all he said was ok. I was beyond elated, I packed my bags and announced to my neighbourhood friends that I was travelling to continue schooling in London.

Departure day arrives, I asked daddy for my passport and he showed it to me. They put my

The Best Laid Plan

luggage into the car along with my Uncle's and we left for Murtala Mohammed International Airport. Everything was going according to plan. But I was not going to let my guard down.

We arrived at the airport and I held onto Uncle Sonny for dear life. We must leave together o, by fire by force. They go through the normal departure procedures and we proceeded to the boarding gates. When we arrived at the gate, my dad and Uncle Sonny went through the charade of saying goodbye. What's my own, I already said goodbyes in the house. Then my dad plays the son card "My dear mother, won't you at least give your son a goodbye hug"? I fell for it! He pulled me to himself and that was it. My plan fell apart from that singular action of falling for emotional blackmail. To see how I cried unashamedly at the airport, you would

In My Father's House

think I was being kidnapped but nobody intervened so it's either they figured out what was happening, or they just didn't care.

Slumped dejectedly at the back of my father's Peugeot station wagon, I wept all the way back to the home I already said goodbye to. I was devastated, I refused to eat. I gave up when the hunger was too hard to endure.

Dad told me the next day that I had made the front page of the Guardian Newspaper. I never saw the paper, so I don't know how true that was. Thankfully, this was before mobile phones and social media. Phew!

The main problem! What do I tell my friends when school resumes? If you ask me, na who I go ask .

CHAPTER 6

Back to School
with Cortina

Do you remember 'Cortina' shoes from back in the day? Those shoes used to be the top 'back to school' footwear in those days. I didn't like them though, I always wanted Mothercare but had no say in the matter of school supplies.

After spending a year writing common entrance exams, I could hang up my pencils. I was tired of shading answers under the watchful eyes of invigilators.

Primary school was finally done and dusted.

I knew my high school destination and I was going to be a Boarder. Yes! (that excitement would be short-lived but that's a story for another book).

We spent most of the holiday preparing for my resumption in High School including buying me a pair of Cortina shoes against my will. By the time September rolled around, my portmanteau had been packed and re-packed several times, but I was ready. To see all the excitement and activity, you would think I was attending school somewhere far. My new school was only about a 10-minute drive from our house and a 5-minute walk from my dad's firm.

Because the hostel didn't open until the

Sunday after school resumption, I would be a day student for the first few days since I lived close enough to attend. My enthusiasm to get the show on the road was intensified by the fact that my favourite guy would be dropping me off on that auspicious first day.

We drove to school and he stopped at the school gate.

"Oya, get down"
"No, you have to take me inside"
"You this child, don't waste my time jare, get down and go into school"
Starting to whine "No, I can't go in by myself"

After about 5 mins of us going back and forth, JOT got down from the car, pulled me out, closed the passenger door, got back in the car and drove off leaving me standing in shock. Me! A whole me! Princess of Obasogun Royal Family.

I quickly looked around to make sure nobody had seen the embarrassing incident and walked off in the direction of my dad's office (not into school). When I got to the junction leading to

his office, I looked left, right, then left again and crossed the dual carriage way then walked into the compound.

Dad did a double-take as I walked into the compound, he couldn't believe his eyes. He looked at me again; saw the pout and determination on my face; my folded arms and probably figured that it was pointless to argue as I was almost late for school. JOT was an authoritative parent who was highly responsive to his child's emotional needs and so he knew to let that fight go. He burst out laughing and said, "You this child, you will not kill me, you were scared to walk into school by yourself, yet bold enough to cross the road and walk down to my office". He then asked his driver to take me back to school, this time, drive me through the gates and make sure that I stayed.

Mission accomplished!

I got what I wanted.... to arrive school in style. I must confess though, with all my bravado earlier in the morning, I had gotten scared the closer we got to school and could not imagine walking into a new school alone. I was only 9 years old after all.

CHAPTER 7

Sunday School

"Train up a child in the way in the way they should go and when he is old, he will not depart from it" – *The Book of Proverbs.*

In my father's house, we went to church – and the whole nine yards. It was non-negotiable. Not only did we have to go to church, but we also had to participate in one way or the other. The family (nuclear and extended) comprised of choir members, altar boys, lay readers, organist etc. When we entered church ehn, everybody knew the Banks had arrived.

Well, my dad also spent a lot of time in the village, which was only about 20 minutes away from town. In his words; "you cannot beat the fresh air and the peace and quiet of the village". All attempts to get me to go with him at non-compulsory periods were an exercise in futility.

We always hoped dad would spend the weekend in the village because it meant we could miss church without him being any wiser. God help you that he doesn't ask what the sermon was about or how Sunday School went. So, he had gone to the village one particular weekend and as the cat was not in the house, the mice came *out to play. Come Sunday, we were all in our various beds basking in the euphoria of not having to go to church when one of my cousins suddenly burst in and jolted us out of our reverie. We all heard it....*

The unmistakable sound of the car horn. The cat had returned unannounced. Wahala! The mice scampered in all directions racing for the bathrooms. By the way, we had only two bathrooms, but we were many mice. Those that could double up, doubled up and those that couldn't, found other ways to get ready (I won't embarrass them by telling you how). But get ready we did and off to church we went. And we had to walk!!!!

Years down the line, I still go to church, whether virtually or physically and I participate wholeheartedly. It is ironic now that I tell my children that going to church is non-negotiable, in my house.

CHAPTER 8

The von Banks Family

"*Music acts like a magic key, to which the most tightly closed heart opens.*"
— Maria von Trapp

We have so far established the following facts:

· JOT loved music
· JOT loved to sing (in church)
· JOT loved church

It can, therefore, be inferred that his children MUST love those things. Right?

Wrong!!!! Back then, it was inconvenient and embarrassing for us to do number 2 and 3 but do it we must.

Daddy would suddenly be inspired to do something, and he would get really excited about it to the detriment of the sensibilities of his dear children. One Sunday, he quickly gathered all of us into his office before service started and taught us one of his favourite hymns and gleefully announced that we would be singing as a family in front of the whole church. Not cool, Pop! Not cool at all. It was not even family Thanksgiving Day. The smiles quickly turned to frowns as we all grumpily went into the church. Jailbreak was not an option!

As the service progressed, we were not invited to sing, and I happily concluded that we escaped Alcatraz that day. Suddenly, the Vicar announced that "The Bankoles will now bless us with a special number". Hian! Diaris God o (There is God). So, we all reluctantly proceeded to the front of the church where dad lined us up according to age and height. Picture that scene in "sound of music" but replace the smiling Von Trapp kids with our grumpy faces.

Sing we did do! His voice was louder than all of us combined. He stood in front of us conducting the singing like the choirmaster that he was, only that the singers were his children. Escape foiled.

Afterwards, me in my head paraphrasing Captain von Trapp: Daddy, is it to be at every church service, or merely this once, that you intend on leading us all through this rare and wonderful new world of…. singing in front of the whole church?

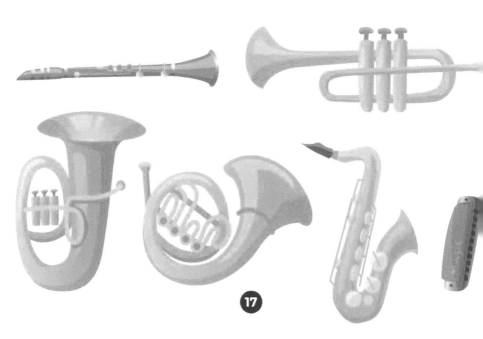

CHAPTER 9

Can't we just Talk this
Through?

"People with highly transferable skills may be specialists in certain areas, but they're also incredible generalists - something businesses that want to grow needs" - Leah Busque.

Sometimes during the holidays, especially when his associates were swamped, JOT would put us to work tendering the fields of Adebayo Bankole & Co Chartered Accountants (AB & Co.) as unpaid audit executives. Well, we got BUKA rice for lunch if that counts as payment. We loved the work and working with figures (I did anyway) and being in the office was the icing on the cake. I also loved the opportunity to play with his secretary's typewriter (when she was not looking). Unbeknownst to me, daddy was paying attention to my office shenanigans.

At the start of one summer holiday, he announced that based on my interest in the typewriter, he was sending me to "Typing and Shorthand" school. What? Can't we just talk this through, Dad?

Dear reader, please understand that my plans this particular summer were to loaf about the house, watch VHS and TV programmes when NEPA permitted and catch up with my friends. It didn't even include 'volunteering' at AB & Co.

The following morning, he ordered me to get ready and we drove to a bookshop to buy supplies for the school. He had that look of determination on his face that dared me to argue so I behaved myself although whining inside. He then drove me to the "school" which wasn't what I was expecting. My expectation was cut short! Why?

The 'school' was more or less a kiosk – one of those small shops in a multicomplex block of shops. Hian! This man does not even like me at all. In my head, I had imagined a posh finishing school which would have made his plan to educate me bearable. Ko le werk! Me, spend two whole months in this place?

He registered me at the school and left for work, silently daring me to defy him. For the next three weeks, I walked to and from the school, was diligent to my learning whilst plotting my escape. By the end of the third week, I'd had enough so I fell 'sick' that weekend. The sickness lasted a week and I never

returned to typing school.

Did JOT make a fuss about me not going back? Not really. He spoke to me in the proverb "Abo oro la nso fun Omoluabi" translated as follows:

 "A word is enough for the wise." – English
"Un mot suffit pour les sages" –French
"EinWortgenügt den Weisen" – German
"Una palabra essuficiente para lossabios" - Spanish

Caveat – I can't speak any of the above languages, it just felt good to translate for emphasis.

To my dad, transferable skills are your greatest asset and once acquired can be applied in any environment. He had a knack for figuring out what skills to send each child to acquire, but we were too carefree to understand his philosophy until much later in life. Some of the things that I am now finding useful were as a result of my dad's insistence on me doing them at an early age.

Should I have stuck with "typewriter" school?

CHAPTER 10

The day I became

"Sisi"

"Before life removed all the innocence"
– Luther Vandross

The song 'Dance with my Father" had always been a favourite of mine. It has also become my go-to song since my dad passed away.

My dad was very playful. He cracked jokes and would laugh even before he finished telling the jokes. He did not lose his sense of humour as he got older and I strongly believe that if his body hadn't aged him, his wit and humour would have kept him young. I remember being carried on his knees or his chest, being tickled and laughing uncontrollably.

I often slept in my mum's room, especially when I was home from boarding school. Every morning, just before he went to work, dad would come into the room, tickle me awake and pull me onto his chest. This was my wakeup call except when he was not at home. This routine continued into my early teenage years.

Until....

One morning, I think I was about 14/15 y/o, he came in as usual and pulled me onto his chest. He hadn't seen me since I returned from boarding school the previous day, so we were happily chatting away. My mum came into the room, looked at us and for some reason, the sight of me on his chest didn't sit right with her that morning (Sorry mum). She said to my dad in annoyance "Ha, JO, se e'mo pe omode yi ti n di sisi nii?" meaning. JO, don't you know this child is becoming a young lady?"

Me? Sisi? Where? How? I was a flat-chested, tomboy at that age. Always climbing trees with my brothers. Sisi was not the right word with which to describe me.

"Words are seeds that do more than blow around. They land in our hearts and not the ground".

That was it, maybe not for my dad but me. I was Sisi and I became self-conscious from then on. No more sleeping on daddy's chest. Luther Vandross got it right with that song. Life indeed removed all the innocence of our daddy-daughter play.

"If I could get another chance
Another walk
Another dance with him
I'd play a song that would never ever end
How I'd love love love
To dance with my father again"

CHAPTER 11

No Time
Wasted

"A man who dares to waste one hour of time has not discovered the value of life" – Charles Darwin.

My dad despised lateness, this was one of his greatest pet peeves. To him, being late was tacky, rude and downright wasteful. There was nothing like 'African time' in JOT's dictionary. Someone invites you to an event, you get there before the start time and before means at least 30 minutes prior.

Since I was his designated handbag, daddy dragged me along to a lot of functions until I wised up to why everyone else disappeared when he was looking for company. One such occasion was the birthday thanksgiving and party of a dear family friend turned Uncle. The event was taking place out of state, so we had left home very early to avoid traffic which meant I didn't have breakfast. We arrived at the church at 9 am for an event starting at 10 am. To quote my dad "Better early than late, this way you get the best seat". I probably spent the whole thanksgiving service daydreaming about the food waiting at the reception and catching up with Uncle's children. I would soon be jolted awake.

When the church service ended, we proceeded to the celebrant's house for the reception and I promptly took my place at one of the well-positioned tables (if you get my drift). Dad was busy exchanging pleasantries with other guests, so all was on track. I was seriously starving by then.

The next thing I heard was "Oya, let's start going".
"Sho! We haven't eaten and I am hungry"
"No, you don't need to eat here, we need to leave so that we can beat the traffic"

The time was 3 pm. This was child endangerment and abuse.

Uncle Taye (his driver at that time) looked at me and burst out laughing "Yetunde, you don't know daddy. He never eats at parties. For him, he has honoured the celebrant by attending the church service then showing face at the reception for a few minutes"

I walked dejectedly to the car and we left real food behind.

When we got on the motorway, dad instructed the Uncle Taye to park by the next corn seller so we could buy boiled corn to hold our tummies. I dealt with the corn as if I had not eaten in over a week as I pondered over my mistake.

CHAPTER 12

Comical
Alektrophobia

"The brave man is not he who does not feel afraid, but he who conquers that fear."
- Nelson Mandela.

Alektorophobia or the fear of chickens is derived from the Greek word 'Elektor' which means 'rooster' and 'Phobos' meaning 'fear.

I knew there had to be a name for it, so I searched google.

My dad had a phobia for live birds, so did I and I think two of my brothers. My phobia started when my little brother was bitten on the face by a mother hen, in my presence. I was only 6 and it was a highly traumatic experience. After that incident, I fled anytime I was around a live bird, including in the market. Unlike the others, I didn't even like to eat chicken not to talk of having the guts to slaughter one for cooking.

Picture this scenario! Mum had asked us to slaughter a chicken and I asked to help out in a bid to overcome the fear. I cut the neck of the bird and thought I was done. Suddenly, the bird gets up with its neck hanging and starts to chase us around the backyard. Yee, insult upon injury. This incident took the phrase " running around like a headless chicken " to a whole new level. Abeg, let me leave the chicken lovers to do all the butchering! After this incidence, we would disappear anytime chicken slaughtering was required in the house.

Anyway, this chapter isn't just about fear of birds but to establish the fact that daddy dearest was a scaredy-cat sometimes. One day, my sister and I (the handbag) accompanied him to visit some friends of his outside of town. The visit went on for hours and we didn't leave for home until after 7 pm. The combination of going through a long and winding road, plus the darkness was already enough to cause my dad some anxiety. A few minutes into the journey, a car suddenly appears behind us and stayed behind us. Dad, being consumed with paranoia, instructed my sister to keep watch of the said car whilst he paid attention to the road and sped up. Some moments later, I started to wonder whether this was my father in the front, driver's seat, or Michael Schumacher racing through the track. After the rather exciting journey –with

my adrenaline-filled father demonstrating his skills at evasion - we ended up back in town, the familiarity and welcoming aura infusing us three with an overwhelming sense of relief as we finally lost the car that was behind us. You never could be too careful those days – if you catch my drift. Whether or not that car was chasing us, or it was just a figment of our suspicious minds remains a mystery till date.

As for me, I have started to conquer my fear of chickens by eating them. Don't ask me to hold one though.

CHAPTER 13

Daddy the
Clairvoyant

As with most Nigerian graduates, I was called up for the compulsory 1-year National Youth Service Corps (NYSC) scheme. According to the decree establishing the scheme, "the purpose of the scheme is primarily to inculcate in Nigerian Youths the spirit of selfless service to the community and to emphasize the spirit of oneness and brotherhood of all Nigerians, irrespective of cultural or social background". In layman's terms, post young graduates to remote locations all over the country, as far as possible from their homes and let their eyes see pepper so they don't become "Lazy Nigerian Youths".

Being curious to see where I would be posted, I did not 'buy' my NYSC posting so was deployed to a state in the North Central region of Nigeria.

When my dad saw the posting, he remembered that one of his distant nieces lived in that state with her family. The only thing was that he did not know where she lived, nor did he have any contact details for her (this was before mobile phones and social media). The only thing he knew for sure was the name of her husband's employer.

Boot camp was to start the following week, so I quickly got ready to travel. I planned to travel via coach on a Monday night to arrive in camp on

Tuesday morning, but my dear father insisted that I travel on Sunday morning. We argued back and forth with me thinking that just because I was an adult, he could not dictate to me. He suddenly said ok, gave me an allowance and left me believing that my plan had prevailed.

Lol! In my dreams ...

Beware, whenever a Nigeria parent suddenly says ok, they have something else in mind.

Dad jolted me out of Lala land on Sunday at 6 am to instruct me to get ready. His driver had arrived to take me to the coach terminal. Hian!

"Daddy, I thought we discussed this; I am not going till tomorrow".
"No, you are going now".

I started to whine as I usually, but his tone of voice suddenly changed "Will you get up my friend? You are going today and that's final".

My brain reset fast. I was 22 but I couldn't have dared to defy my very Nigerian father at that moment. I grumpily got up, got ready and they dropped me off at the coach terminal.

As the journey got underway, I uncharacteristically struck up conversations with a woman and her toddler and with two fellow 'Corpers'. Due to unexpected delays, the journey took longer than planned and when it became obvious that we would arrive at our destination very late, the nice woman offered us (me and the two other "corpers") a place to sleep overnight before proceeding on the final leg of our journey to boot camp the following day. Whilst we were preparing to leave the next morning, the conversation led to the woman stating that her husband knew every Yoruba person that worked at the company where my cousin's husband worked. I mentioned the surname and the woman screamed in excitement that she knew the couple personally and would take me to their house. We said goodbye to the other "corpers" and she took me to my cousin's place. What happened afterwards was surreal, but I eventually ended up at boot camp on Tuesday like I initially planned.

After Bootcamp, I got back home and told daddy dearest all that had transpired. He said "I said it, would you have located your cousin if I had not insisted that you leave on Sunday? What an adult can see, a child cannot begin to comprehend."

"I haf hear".

Sometimes I ask myself if it was all just a coincidence or if he actually "knew". There were many instances like that where he demonstrated incredible foresight that it's hard not to believe he knew things.

Lines falling in pleasant places more like.

CHAPTER 14

Still on the NYSC Matter

I once authored a book. It was during NYSC service year and an appraisal of the scheme. The person that wrote the foreword for that book will write the foreword for this one, but he doesn't know it yet. Chris and I met at Bootcamp then we both ended up arranging redeployment to a South West state for the rest of our service year. He teased me a lot at Bootcamp but also gave me a crash course in volleyball when I had to play for my platoon.

Anyway, I wrote the book and my dad proudly and lovingly published it. His special skill was encouraging his children and being actively involved in whatever concerns us so he decides that we should hold a book launch and invite a notable personality (aka State Governor) to the launch. However, he wasn't going to help me lobby the governor to attend, I had to do that all by myself. It was a lesson in independence and resilience.

I started the lobbying process and must have gone to the Governor's office like ten times (no kidding) before I finally got in to see him. Unfortunately, he was booked for the launch date (he gave me a tidy little sum as his contribution) but suggested I contacted his first lady and so began my next journey. I eventually got the first lady's office to commit then told my dad to print the invitation cards which I quickly distributed.

All through my lobbying process, I had tried to see the NYSC director for the state to no avail, so I ended up leaving the invitation card for them.

The weekend before the launch, I walked into the NYSC directorate and saw a small gathering of the top executives. I walked towards them still in my little bubble thinking I would finally get to talk to the director.

My bubble burst!

It was the invitation that was being discussed and the moment I came into view, the director started to scream about how they would make sure I repeated my service year. I quickly went down on both knees begging. Haa, what did I do?

I had broken protocol. I had gone directly to the state governor behind their back and without their permission. If only they knew what I went through sef!

I left the directorate in tears, walked to the nearest telecommunications office, bought a phone card and called my daddy. I narrated the whole saga to him, and his response was. "Wipe your tears, my dear, we shall resolve this matter". He asked me a few questions to establish some facts and said he would get back to me over the weekend.

When my dad makes a promise, I trust him wholeheartedly. He never disappoints.

When launch day arrived, the director not only attended the event, but they gave a nice speech about how I was well brought up and even when they were furious at me, I quickly knelt to apologise etc. By the end of the launch, they and my dad had become buddies.

How did he do it? I know but I am not telling.

CHAPTER 15

Water Pressure does not

Kill Fish

––––––––

"You are never too young to learn, never too old to change" –
Russell M. Nelson.

For my dad, education was non-negotiable, formal or informal. The man was brilliant and knew a bit about every topic there was. No Kidding! Although he was a chartered accountant, he once articulated the intricacies of civil engineering and bridge design to my nine-year-old self.

As an accountant, he was a walking calculator and I got my love of and for numbers from him. This did not mean that he expected everyone to be as brilliant (if not more) as he was but it meant he could recognise some form of genius in all his wards. He had files for each of the children in his household; every report, every activity was carefully filed away after a detailed review and action plan. He would also pit us against each other once in a while just to challenge us. He said to me once that my little brother was more brilliant than I was after the boy beat my record from a previous grade. Yee Mogbe, 'impossicant' I must do better next time.

For me, his brilliance meant that he pushed me academically (more like tortured me at that time). I was almost 13, just starting my 4th year in high school when I wrote my first GSCE exams. My older brother and his friends wrote the same exams and I was 'fortunate' to be in the same exam centre and hall with one of his friends who let me copy him when we had the same papers. Whether I copied right or wrong, I ended up with 7 passes and 1 fail. You should have seen my dad's excitement at the very woeful result. All he saw was potential; he said: "Great job, you will do it again next year". The following year, I wrote the exams again and did very well, enough to get me into University except I was too young. My birth certificate mysteriously disappeared when I was going into University that we had to swear an affidavit to confirm my age. I think it was more my book smarts that saw me through school than my emotional intelligence (not sure I had any).

Towards the end of my course and into NYSC year, we started planning my master's programme abroad. Daddy had done a lot of research and pulled forms for as many top universities as he could find, and we started to submit applications for scholarships. I was so certain that I would get a scholarship for one top university as we had gone

through a rigorous selection process to the final stage but that was not to be. The day the final letter came, my dad had driven down to my place of primary assignment in another state to break the news personally. Previously, he would phone me up but this time, he wanted to be there to provide emotional support. I was very upset, but his eternal optimism lifted my spirits that day. Well, he could not afford the fees at that time, so we had to decline the admission offer (without scholarship) and I decided to enter the employment market instead.

Years down the line, I am in a stand-off with my daughter:
"I don't know why you are making me do all these things, it's too much"
"You are fortunate it's just this when I was your age ....
"Yes, I know, I know, grandpa made you write GCSE at 13"
My phone rings "See, it's your grandpa... daddy, please tell this child how much you made me study"
"Hello, Tosho my darling, don't mind your mummy, ok? I know you are a very smart child"

Grandparents are the worst. I rest my case.

CHAPTER 16

Doors of
Opportunities

"If opportunity doesn't knock, build a door" - Milton Berle.

After the scholarship application fell through, I started to look for paid employment. As you can imagine, I was late to the party as my fellow corpers started attending interviews whilst we were serving our motherland.

It was the days of snail mail, there were no online applications, so I had to go submit my CV directly at different companies. Don't even think about the postal service if you wanted results. If you were fortunate enough to know one uncle who knew one aunty who had one friend at the company, you might get a callback.

So was the life of a job seeker in those days. Daddy paved the way for me at a few places but apart from that, I had to commute daily to look for work. It was practically an 8 am to 5 pm grind through the streets of Lagos.

One of the earliest callbacks I received was from one of the big 4 international audit firms. Unfortunately, by the time the invitation to test arrived in the post, the interview date had passed. Arghhhh! Not to worry. Daddy dove into his treasure trove of business cards, pulled out the card he wanted, wrote a short note and sent me with the note to the recipient who happened to be a senior manager at the said audit firm. I set out on this 'errand' about midday and arrived at the firm about 2 pm, eventually seeing the man at about 3 pm. When I told him who had sent me, he was so excited and spent the next 20 minutes telling me how my dad had trained him many years before when JOT was a senior partner at their predecessor firm. He finally gets to the point of my visit and called another senior colleague to ask for his help then sent me on my way to a different office location. I got to the other location at about 6 pm and it turned out that this other colleague too was trained by my dad. He immediately told HR to run the test for me that evening. Oh Lord, help me! Well, I did not pass that test – it was an annoying test asking me to name the currencies of many countries that I had not even been to- so that chapter closed but the whole episode reminded me that a good man's deed lives on after him.

A few months after, I wrote and passed a proper test with one of the Banks, got the job, had my induction and was posted to one of the branches as a Teller. I was keeping my head down doing my job when I got a call from one of the Bank's Regional directors.

"Is this Yetunde Bankole?"
"Yes Sir"
"I understand you know the managing director of company X here in State Y and can

introduce us to him"
"Ermmmm... Yes Sir"
"Ok then, we will arrange how to bring you over so we can have a meeting with him"

I hung up slowly, confused. What just happened? How did he know my connection to that company? There is a mole in my life.

Well, turns out the mole was my dad. I got home that weekend and before I could ask, he brought out the copy of the 'lovely' letter he had written to the Bank's managing director whom he didn't know personally by the way. The general gist of the letter was to thank the Bank for employing his very brilliant daughter bla bla bla and how I have connections that could bring in deposits into the Bank. Yee! Daddy has finished me finally.

Have you heard about the power of P.I.E in organisation progression?
P – Performance
I – Image
E - Exposure

Exposure is who knows you and who has seen you in action and can speak on your behalf when you're not in the room and decisions need to be made around things like promotion, progress etc, "Who will be your greatest champion at the big table?"

In hindsight, this was my dad helping me to get some exposure and build a door of opportunities. That conversation with the regional director was the start of some form of mentorship throughout my time at the Bank.

CHAPTER 17

Headed in The Right

Direction

"The best way to predict the future is to create it." —Abraham Lincoln.

JOT had high hopes that I would train as a medical doctor and I did apply to study medicine but unfortunately did not meet the cut-off marks for admission, so I settled for chemical sciences. Good thing I changed course though, I probably wouldn't have loved being a medical doctor. As it turned out, I loved chemistry and as one of my lecturers used to say, "what is not chemistry?" Even love alludes to chemistry.

During my 200L at university, dad was appointed as a member of the board of

the state university teaching hospital and he concluded that this was the opportunity to make me a doctor as he wanted. He had it all planned out, I would complete my 200Level courses and do a direct entry into medical school. He said to me as if he was comforting me, "Don't worry, you'll be done with medical school by age 29. By this point, I knew to only look and nod as there was no point arguing with him when he gets his teeth sunk into an idea. However, thanks to lecturers' strikes, by the time I graduated, he had forgotten the medical school plan and we shifted to Master's. Besides, he was no longer a board member at said school.

36

With my BSc in chemical sciences, I could only get a job in banking as the banks were the only ones employing smart scientists like me back then. No shaking, we go with the flow as usual. After I started working, dad immediately adjusted his plans to me becoming a chartered accountant like he was. He reminded me at every opportunity that I should write the exams to no avail. He then directed his mentoring efforts to my friends and would then use their collection of successes to try to manipulate me, forgetting that he had raised me to think independently.

Many years later, I decided to undertake my MSc. Programme in the UK and as expected, Pop was over the moon. He made it a point of duty to phone me at least once a week whilst I was in school. One day, after our usual chit chat, he went suddenly quiet. I swear, I could hear the wheels turning in his head. He finally said, "My dear mother, after you finish this MSc., you continue to a PhD in Finance. You never know, you might be the next Ngozi Okonjo-Iweala (the then Minister of Finance of Nigeria)". I wanted to respond with "Hian! You've come again o, you won't let me rest", but what I said instead was, "Ok daddy, I will think about it".

To be fair, I did think about it, it just wasn't feasible for me to do a PhD at that time, so I took a job instead. Trust my father to find the positive in that decision. This time, his dream – which has now been realised in his absence- turned into seeing me work in the UK civil service then public service. He believed in public service as he loved to serve people, he was a man of the people. I cried the day I got the civil service offer because he never got to see his dream fulfilled.

Cheers to you dad, one down, many more to go! Maybe I will do that PhD for you eventually. Let me make some millions first.

CHAPTER 18

Father of the

Bride

"You fathers will understand. You have a little girl. An adorable little girl who looks up to you and adores you in a way you could never have imagined. I remember how her little hand used to fit inside mine" – George Banks in Father of the Bride movie.

I love that movie and its sequel. George and Annie have that special father-daughter bond too. In fact, a conversation like the below ensued between my dad and I when we were planning my wedding.

George: You know, that's not a bad idea. Who else can we ask not to eat? My parents and your mother.
Annie: Why don't we just charge people? That way we can make money on the wedding.

My dad was a classic Fatherzilla (if that word exists) who questioned every expense. But like in the movie, he ended up paying for the wedding anyway.

As traditional as JOT was, he made the decision that I should get married in the city where I worked instead of back home at his local congregation. He reasoned that all my friends lived in that city and it would be unfair to bring them to our home city two days in a row, so he immediately called the diocesan Bishop and booked the date.

On the day of the wedding, my dad put everybody in every available vehicle including his own and left them with strict instructions not to be late for the church service then walked to the bus park to jump on "Danfo" bus with his flowing agbada. As was the norm on Saturday mornings, there was a traffic jam on the way to church, so JOT got down from the bus, removed his agbada and folded it then flagged down an 'Okada' to take him to the church. He got to church at 9 am for a wedding that was to start at 11 am. Hian! He was the father of the bride after all.

I had slept at my Uncle's house the night before the wedding so that I could be close to the church. Unfortunately, this meant that timekeeper daddy couldn't directly drag me out of this house, but he chased me via phone till I arrived at 10 am. Imagine! Story of my life.

By the way, Anglican churches are a stickler for time, they will start the service without the celebrant if need be, so I do understand why he fussed about punctuality. Being always punctual is very stressful though.

"Punctuality is the virtue of the bored" – Evelyn Waugh

What is wrong with being fashionably late? You didn't hear that from me o.

CHAPTER 19

I Am Not in

"There is no friendship, no love, like that of the parent for the child."
– Henry Ward Beecher.

I am not in denial that my dad was not a perfect human being, but his great personality, humility and overwhelming optimism overshadowed his many faults. We no doubt had many cat and mouse episodes. According to a popular Yoruba adage, the teeth that a lioness uses to play with its child is the same one she bites the child with. That was the case when my dad and I had our lioness and cub moments - the rod of correction was put to good use and when I became too old for the rod, word (s) of correction took its place.

There were times when I concluded that I hated the man - which child does not have those moments - and took regrettable actions to express my extreme emotions. However, no matter how extreme I became or how much I broke his heart or how angry he got with me, his love always covered my multitude of sins. The unconditional love of my earthly father made it very easy for me to accept the love of my heavenly father.

As I journeyed into maturity, the hardest transition I made was a detachment from certain beliefs that my parents held. This did not go down so well as JOT was a very traditional man but our views on the current relevance of some traditions didn't necessarily match up. I learnt, after many missteps, how to disagree with my parents whilst also keeping the biblical instructions to honour them.

We named my first daughter three days after she was born, in the hospital, with no fuss, just a couple of pastors and friends who happened to be visiting at that time. After we got home and my dad came to visit, I handed the baby to him and said,

"Meet your granddaughter, Rotimi". He didn't react visibly, but I knew my dad enough to tell that he was disappointed. A week later, on the day that would have been traditionally the naming ceremony, daddy sent a text message to me that would forever be engraved in my memory:

"In accordance with the custom and tradition of the Yoruba people, my brother, Chief O.A Bankole, hereby

name your beautiful baby girl, Omotosho."
Omotosho means a child is like (or as good as/up to) a jewel. A lot of love had gone into choosing that name, it was as uncommon as it was beautiful, but trust me to be dismissive. I got to know later that my dad had ordered a live ram to butcher for the naming ceremony, but he returned it as the ceremony didn't take place. I didn't understand what I had done until much later; I had dishonoured him; I had denied him the chance to properly celebrate the birth of his first biological granddaughter in the way that mattered to him. He never stopped calling her 'Omotosho', he would sometimes fondly shorten it to Tosho.

After that episode, I learnt to 'Give unto Caesar what is Caesar's, even when our views didn't necessarily align. Part of the process of maturing is balancing open-mindedness with standing firm in your convictions.'

CHAPTER 20

Prince
Charming

"You know what charm is: a way of getting the answer 'yes' without having asked any clear question." – Albert Camus.

Have you ever encountered someone who was positively charming? You possibly couldn't put your finger on it, but there was simply something about them that made you want to be around them. You hang onto every word they say and could literally stick your fingers in a fire if they told you it was ok to do so, just because they were so irresistible. JOT was in that class of someone.

As part of the funeral arrangements, we held a tribute night in dad's honour. He had positively impacted so many lives and we wanted to capture as many views on camera as possible. The person that set the ball rolling that night was a vicar turned politician who jokingly ended his speech with a sneaky "JOT loved his women". That comment drew a lot of nods and laughs and nearly became the rhetoric for the evening with my mum also drawing on it in her own speech. When my siblings and I took the stage, I told the audience one of my daddy episodes as follows:

Dad and I were watching TV together and the news came on about a now

Late Nigerian statesman, Chief W. My dad shook his head and said: "Bobo yi o fine rara sha" meaning this guy is not fine at all. I started to laugh uncontrollably and said to him "You know both of you have one thing in common, wives (plural). The only difference is the women were probably attracted to his money, but your charm is your selling point, daddy". He playfully pulled his flip flops and threw it at me and said "O ba Iya e" – back at your mother.

JOT was not a very tall man, a fact that would probably have disqualified him in my generation that was all about tall, dark and handsome men. Fortunately, the next generation of Bankole males -aka my brothers and cousins got the tall genes from our grandfather.

What he lacked in height, he made up for in spades of wit and charm. Daddy could charm the socks of a child. He had this charisma that made meeting him for the first time feel like you had known him forever. A friend of mine said, "Yetunde, your house was the only one where all of us felt very comfortable to be ourselves. Your dad pulled us in like we were his kids".

My dad didn't just talk the talk but backed up his words with real actions and his promises with deeds that showed he wasn't just out to further himself – he wanted the best for those around him. He taught me the value of paying it forward. You would have loved him if you had met him.

Are you impressed yet?

CHAPTER 21

Two Peas in a *Pod*

"When brothers agree, no fortress is so strong as their common life." – Antisthenes

My uncle, Otunba O.A Bankole, the other surviving son of my paternal grandmother, passed away whilst I was writing this book so I decided to write this chapter. The last time I saw him was when I travelled home for my dad's funeral, but I am glad I got a chance to see him briefly. In our community, JOT was a man of the people whilst Otunba was the strong pillar quietly moving chess pieces across the board.

Otunba and JOT were brothers like I have never seen. Their fortress of brotherhood was so strong that it was both enviable and scary. My dad never did anything without express approval from his older brother. Once upon a time, dad decided that he wanted to sell one of his properties but we didn't want him to, so we reported the matter to Otunba who then instructed my cousin to go to the property and tag the whole place with a caveat emptor, "This property is not for sale". Daddy was furious when he saw the tag, he went haywire on us until we told him that his brother authorised it. His anger immediately petered out, he fumed for days but the plan to sell was dead. Otunba had spoken!

The day before he suffered the stroke that eventually led to his passing, he had snuck to the village to say happy birthday to his brother. That was the last time they were physically in each other's presence. Whilst he was recuperating in the hospital, JOT would insist on talking to "Boda mi" as he fondly called Otunba, so he could set his mind at rest. Boda mi too wouldn't rest until he spoke with Taiye. Two months later, JOT took a bow.

When JOT passed away, the decision was made not to tell Otunba as everyone was worried about the outcome, so he was only told a few days to the funeral (3 months afterwards). We believe he sensed that something was amiss as he kept asking after his brother so just to buy some time; he was told that we had flown him abroad for treatment.

I called Otunba shortly after he was informed of JOT's passing, and I could feel the heartbreak in his voice. We spoke for a few minutes then he said to me "Taiye ti fi iku s'egbon bayi" meaning, "Taiye has now become the older one by dying first". For his sake, I held my tears until I got off the phone. I

remembered how whenever I visited him in town, dad would insist (sometimes unsuccessfully) that I go visit "Boda mi" in the village. He would say, "You know he is getting older; you don't know how long we would have him for". What an irony!

After my dad's funeral events, Otunba said: "I am not wicked so I will not go now, I will give you guys a few months". He lived true to his word and died ready, surrounded by family.

The general sentiment now is what would happen to the community with the exit of these two great men who poured their heart and soul into community development. It is the end of an era but not the end of their legacy.

CHAPTER 22

A Legacy of Character

and Faith

The greatest legacy one can pass on to one's children and grandchildren is not money or other material things accumulated in one's life, but rather a legacy of character and faith.
—Billy Graham

Thank you for walking down memory lane with me and hope you have enjoyed seeing my dad through my eyes. Writing this book has been a mixture of giggles, laughter, tears and gratitude for me and everyone that has helped to put these pages together. The stories are by no means exhaustive; I just didn't want to bore you by writing too many chapters.

At the end of the events celebrating my dad's life, I was a very proud daughter. They say people never speak ill of the dead, but I say you can usually tell what is made up and what is real. There were many reports of his positive contributions into so many lives. Stories of how he used his personal funds to build school blocks, how he lobbied the government to make sure his community was taken care of etc. Beyond the illness he had later in life, what killed my dad was his fight for justice in his hometown.

46

We, his children, were consistently implored at all the different events to carry on his legacy of character and faith. He loved people, his community and most of all, his church.

Is it possible to fill the vacuum he left? Probably not, but we will certainly try.

What legacy are you leaving your children? How will your children remember you? Will it be a legacy of character and faith—a legacy that shares of God's goodness.

Printed in Great Britain
by Amazon